Just Beyond THE VEIL

Stories of Death and Dying, Grief and Loss

Kate Sophia Brennan Anderson

From far, from eve and morning
And yon twelve winded sky,
The stuff of life to knit me
Blew hither: here am I.

Now-for a breath I tarry
Nor yet disperse apart-
Take my hand quick and tell me,
What have you in your heart.

Speak now, and I will answer:
How shall I help you, say:
Ere to the wind's twelve quarters
I take my endless way.

"A Shropshire lad"

A.E. Houseman

From Mary Teberg, M.D,. on August 8, 1980

New Energy Press
1210 County Road 39 NW
Monticello, MN 55362

ISBN: 1441426795
ISBN-13: 9781441426796

9 8 7 6 5 4 3 2 1

First Edition
Printed in the United States of America

Library of Congress Cataloging-in-Publication Data
Kathleen Marie Brennan Anderson, 2010
Just Beyond the Veil: A Manual for Living with Death and Dying
Kathleen Marie Brenna Anderson—1st Ed.
p. cm.
ISBN 9780964297920
1. Death and dying. 2. Grief and bereavement. 3. Spirituality.

This manual is dedicated to my parents, Bob and Lee, and to my soul mate and partner in crime, Bill. Without his love, good humor, and patience this manual would never have been written. And, of course, to all of my patients, their friends and families who have shared their hearts and souls with me and been my teachers throughout my life.

PROLOGUE

I was the second of five children in my family. My mother was a nurse, and my father was a pilot for Northwest Airlines. When my mother was seven months pregnant she found a lump in her breast. Her Catholic physicians at the time were reluctant to remove the lump for fear of harming the baby. Thus, directly after she delivered a baby boy, it was determined that she had breast cancer involving the lymph nodes, and she had a mastectomy. Before she was able to leave the hospital, she also had a total hysterectomy.

While Dad was away on flights, I became Mom's companion, accompanying her to doctor appointments, radiation, and the like. She was realistic and yet positive with all of us, telling us that Dad was not one to live alone, and he had her blessing to marry again. It seemed incomprehensible to me that God would take away a young mother with five children to raise. She died four years later, and life as we knew it would never be the same.

Working as a young nurse in the hospital, I gravitated toward patients who were very ill or dying, and I requested to care for them each day that I worked. I believe I was comfortable with them because of my experience of helping my mother. These patients were often relegated to the very end of the wing; this was before Hospice was available. Walking into their rooms, I saw their wide eyes and sensed the fear and isolation they must have felt and I quickly learned that people who are dying do not have the time, strength, nor breath to waste if one was not able to meet them where they were. I sensed that it was sacred, precious time.

My experience with loss deepened after I married and had four miscarriages. With each pregnancy I was sent to bed and then miscarried at around four months. I remember the deep sadness, frustration, and loss of dreams that I felt. You can imagine my elation when our son was born healthy and full term. Not long after that, we moved to Connecticut, where I discovered the Roncalli Institute for Hospice and Homecare. Founded by a priest from Northern Ireland, Father Ed, and a former nun and psychologist from southern Ireland, Siobahn, I felt I found a home. Here my formal Hospice training began, as I learned about maintaining healthy boundaries, the art and science of pain control, and how to deal with patients and families who often were anguished. If Siobahn felt any one of us was overextended, she would call us into her office "for a little one on one." My experiences there were enlightening.

My sister Jeanne was five years younger than I. We shared a bedroom and our love of horses. We pooled our babysitting money in the hopes that one day we would be able to buy a horse. We were, as Jeanne used to say, "best friends AND sisters!" After Mom died, acquiescing to her request, Dad moved us out to our farm in the country. It could not have been easy, raising five kids and making a living while managing his work schedule. One day Jeanne and I presented our little pile of money we had saved to buy a horse, and Dad pulled through and actually bought two for us so we could ride together. We were inexperienced riders at best, and the horses taught us every trick they knew to buck us off or bite us. It mattered little–we were in heaven! When she was only thirteen, Jeanne had a major psychic break and was diagnosed with paranoid schizophrenia. After that her life became a roller coaster ride with periods of lucidity, but longer periods that became more and more bizarre. When she was forty, she died of poisoning. The devastation I felt seemed to have no end. I could not understand how the world could keep turning when Jeanne was gone.

Not long after that, I had a healing by Echo Bodine, an author, psychic, and healer. She told me I had the gift of healing and that it was time to learn about it. My skepticism knew no bounds—no hocus pocus for me! She urged me to check out classes that were offered. I found my way to Pathways, a center for healing in south Minneapolis. Sitting on the couch reading brochures for classes, a radiant barefoot woman with long wavy hair approached me and took the brochures out of my hands. "Stand up!" she said, taking both of my hands in hers. It felt that electricity flowed in my hands and arms, then through my body. Never had I experienced anything like it! She said, "You have the gifts of healing, of loving, and giving. It is time for you to learn about them." I stood there, bewildered, as she moved on to another person. The next day I returned to Pathways to find out who the mystery woman was.

John, the receptionist, was seated at the desk. Who is she? I asked. John had a quizzical look as he replied, "I was here all day and I don't remember seeing any-one like that!" I began to explore alternative medicine, including the healing arts, which brings me to life today, many years later.

INTRODUCTION

In indigenous and other cultures, children grow up witnessing the cycle and interconnectedness of life. Elders live with their families, and are loved and respected. Children learn early that death is a doorway, a transition, not something to be feared. The success of TV shows such as CSI Reality Shows and the Sopranos bring death into our living rooms, and we experience it somewhat vicariously.

But in our society, death is denied and youth is worshipped. Many of us live our lives feeling immortal. Some of us are baby boomers, and we fight the aging process any way we can. No matter what, life is unpredictable and in these uncertain times post 911 and Hurricane Katrina, the war in Afghanistan and Iraq. One visit to the doctor with devastating news, we are all are vulnerable, no matter our age.

Who do we turn to, how do we begin? Family and friends are on the front lines, of course, but it takes a village to get through devastating times. Wonderful organizations, including churches can be counted on to help. "Caring Bridge" and "Share the Care" group enlists individuals to bring meals, drive to doctor appointments, do laundry, or whatever the afflicted person needs help with. Whether it is our own transition or that of a friend or loved one, we want the process from life to death to be as meaningful as it can be. We can access all the wisdom, love, and support available to us in this world as well as the one that lies just beyond the veil of this existence.

What is the veil, exactly, and why is it important? Ancient cultures share a belief that a veil that we cannot see separates this world from the next. The deceased people who have loved us, our friends and families, who have been close to us, want to help us, and are just beyond the veil of this world that we live in. All we have to do to access all the love, support, wisdom, and help available to each one of us is to ask.

I do personal rituals as I prepare to work with my clients. I make certain I feel grounded to the earth. This is as simple as placing my feet flat on the floor, taking a few cleansing breaths, and imagining roots going from the soles of my feet deep into the earth. I connect to the elements–east, west, south, and north–and ask that each of the elements send their essence to the home of the clients I will see that day. The essence of north is the earth itself, trees, rocks, and deep grounding. The essence of east is air and light–the dawn of each new day bringing infinite possibilities and new beginnings. The essence of south is about fire, passion and love, tenacity, courage, and the image of the phoenix rising from the ashes. The direction of west is about the power of water, emotions and the moon. Finally I ask to release any attachments to outcomes that I have. Once I reach my first destination, I wash my hands and ask to release any stress of the day, so that I may be fully present. Then I am ready to begin.

As a Hospice and home care nurse for more than forty years, it has been my honor and privilege to care for people who are approaching the end of life. They have been my teachers, and have become a part of me. I remember their smiles and the unique essence of each individual. My life has been immeasurably enriched because of them. They have taught me what miracles the dying can achieve in those final weeks, days, and hours–for themselves and for those they leave behind. I invite you to come along with me. Learn from the legacy left by my patients, as we share their stories.

CONTENTS

PART I: MAKING PEACE

CHAPTER 1 Chad's Story

It is the Human touch in this world that counts,
The touch of your hand and mine,
Which means far more
Than shelter and bread and wine;
For shelter is gone when the night is over,
And bread lasts only a day,
But the touch of your hand, and the sound of your
voice
Sing on in my soul always.

Spencer Michael Free

I met Chad in late summer, not long before his thirty-fifth birthday. A tall, slender man with a twinkle in his brown eyes, Chad was an avid outdoorsman and a skilled carpenter who also loved to putter in his garage. Chad's illness seemed innocuous enough at first. He came down with a flu bug that refused to go away. Weeks passed. Then months later, he was able to do little more than get up from the couch. His legs were weak and he had no appetite or energy. A battery of tests proved inconclusive and he was treated for depression. He reported having double vision, and he learned that Multiple Sclerosis or an elusive malignancy were possible explanations.

With Chad unable to return to work, the stress at home escalated. He and Naomi had two active boys, ages five and seven. Despite herself, between her demanding, full-time job and acting as a solo parent, she became resentful of her "lump of a husband on the couch." Eventually, Chad's health deteriorated to the point where he needed a wheelchair and could no longer manage at home, which is where I came in. His fine motor skills had become affected as well as his speech. His mind was clear and he was acutely aware of the changes in his body. Naomi spent evenings with her friends and slept on the couch.

The tension in the home was palpable. Understandably, Chad became very upset that no one could determine what was causing a strong, thirty-four-year-old man to deteriorate. Shortly after I met him, he said, "I'm dying and no on knows why!" Friends who visited sat on the couch looking at the floor, unsure of what to say. After a while, they stopped coming. Chad spoke of feeling isolated and adrift—watching his marriage and his life slip through his fingers. His birthday was quickly approaching, and we tried to coax him to think of some kind of food that sounded good to him. He finally broke out in a big grin and said, "Pizza!"

Chad's birthday landed on a perfect summer day, and he wanted to eat his pizza on the deck. The air was soft and warm, and bees were abundant. Due to his loss of fine motor function, he had trouble closing his fingers to hold a utensil. We watched as he managed to hold a piece of pizza in his hand, and slowly and sporadically move it to his open mouth. Just then, a bee landed and decided that pizza would make a great lunch, too. Chad frowned and moved his other hand with two cupped fingers toward the bee. He got it and that was the end of the bee as he muttered, "MY pizza."

I vividly recall one trip to the neurologist's office, not long after I entered the picture. Chad asked the doctor in halting speech, "Am I dying? Why can't you do something to help me?"

The physician turned aside and took Naomi into the hall while I stayed behind. Chad wept, saying, "It's MY life! He should be talking to ME!" After a few moments they both returned. The doctor simply told Chad there was nothing more he could for him, and abruptly left.

Chad wept uncontrollably all the way home. Shortly after we got there, Naomi returned to work, and I sat on the bed, holding his hand. Chad was quiet for a while and then asked, "Kate do you care for me?" I told him that of course I did. "If you care for me, then give me some pills."

I felt shaken. To witness the deterioration of this human being was devastating enough and I was not prepared for his request. "Help me die, help me die," Chad sobbed. This was the first time I had been confronted about my boundaries in this way. I could empathize with the place that Chad was in, and if the tables were turned, I too might have hoped someone would assist me. I felt torn and powerless to help Chad. After a while, he became more peaceful and told me what he intended to do. He had decided that he could no longer eat anything in solid form, and asked if I would honor this decision. I said I would.

Frequently the little boys would sit on my lap next to Chad's bed. They told me about their day at school or we read stories. Chad seemed to enjoy this as much as the boys did. One afternoon I was rubbing Chad's back when Mike, the youngest, came in and asked, "What are you doing?" I told him I was trying to make his dad feel better. He asked if he could help and, with Chad's permission, I showed him how. Mike crawled on the bed to be close to his dad, and with great tenderness and intensity, rubbed his daddy's back. Tears rolled down Chad's face. Soon Jake came in the room and wanted to help, too. They both kept this up for nearly ten minutes before plopping on the bed to snuggle. I told them what good work they did, and how it must have helped to make their dad feel better. Chad nodded "yes."

It took nearly two weeks after Chad stopped eating for him to die. Toward the end, it became more and more important for us to anticipate his needs and understand his garbled speech. He simply didn't have the energy to repeat his words. The stress for Naomi seemed unbearable. Chad frequently lashed out at whoever was near, and Naomi often bore the brunt of this.

One day Chad awakened from sleep and asked to call Naomi home right away. I asked him whether he was leaving us, but he said, "No." Naomi rushed home and spent over an hour in their room together, with the door closed that when the door opened I noticed something had changed. They both looked radiant. Later, I learned from Naomi they had connected in some special place where there was no shame and no blame. I was reminded of a quote from Rumi, "There is a field out beyond right and wrong doing. I will meet you there." They forgave each other, she told me. For what, she didn't say. But I did learn that their conversation dealt with their entire relationship, not just the time after Chad became ill. Was the letting go of old grievances transformational for them? I believe it was and I know Naomi thought so too.

Chad's peace didn't last. Each day after that felt like a roller coaster of emotions, and people who only wanted to help seemed to get in the way. The minister came, but we heard a cry of "GET OUT!" not long after he arrived. As the man hurriedly left the room, I ran in to find Chad sobbing. It seemed there was so little we could do to make him comfortable. The only thing we could do was BE with him. There was no cure, no release of his anguish. Even so, he wanted us to stay by the bed, sometimes holding his hand, sometimes not. Our vigil continued. I believe that he felt our love, compassion, and empathy as we walked with him as far as we could on his journey.

I was not present when Chad died, but his family described to me what happened. They stood in a circle around his bed, holding hands and watching him as his respirations became further and further apart. Finally they ceased altogether, and Chad's face reflected that he was at peace. The family stayed at his bedside for over two hours, touching him and softly talking to him. Finally, when they were ready to release his body, they contacted the funeral home. Their emotions ran high as Chad's body was removed, and they held one another as they wept.

After Chad died, I was relieved that he finally was at peace, but it felt odd not to be interacting with his family. It was devastating to witness the loss of this young husband, father, and son.

I felt a physical ache in my chest, and tears fell freely. Unfortunately at the time, my husband could not provide me with support. I believe he felt threatened by the bond that quickly forms between a nurse and patient, not just with Chad. I found solace with colleagues at work, and my therapist. Walking in the woods and journaling also helped immensely, and soon I was ready to fully engage again.

On my father's farm, next to the barn, is a path that leads to a meadow that has been my spiritual habitat for many years. One night not long after Chad died, I had a vivid dream. As I walked along the long lane heading to the house, I saw a man leaning on the fence by the barn, his back toward me, gazing up at the meadow. He was dressed in a flannel plaid shirt, jeans, and boots. I watched the tall, lanky stranger, wondering who it could be. As I approached, he turned to greet me, arms outstretched to give me a big hug and smile. It was Chad— fit, healthy, and whole. He kept his arm around me and turned us to face the meadow. "If you ever need me, I'm here for you." Then I awakened. To this day I remember every detail of that dream.

THOUGHTS...

Chad modeled something very important for all of us. He lost control over his body, and ultimately his life. The anger and sadness never left him. Regardless, he maintained control in significant ways. He chose when to let go of life, although he was not allowed to have pills to end his life when he wanted them. Despite the fact that he yelled at the people he needed the most, it did not mean he didn't love them. He chose to allow those he loved to nurture him, and to participate in a process of forgiveness with his wife.

The talk Chad initiated about forgiveness surely was not easy for him, vulnerable as he was. The motivation to do it must have been great, and the benefits intuitive. I saw the results on their faces. Earlier, Chad shared with me that he did not want his life or his marriage with Naomi to end on a sad, bitter note. After their talk, I could see the love they had for each other had been rekindled.

CHAPTER 2 Don's Story

When I am dead, cry for me a little, think of me sometimes but not too much. It's not good for you to allow your thoughts to dwell too long upon the dead. Think of me now and again, as I was in life, at some moment which is pleasant to recall, but not for too long. Leave me in peace, as I shall leave you in peace. While you live, let your thoughts be with the living.

Native American Ishi of the Pacific Northwest

A tall, burly man with jet black hair and a beard, Don was only forty years old when a tsunami of events and emotions broke upon him. In quick succession, he was diagnosed with a brain tumor, separated from his children, divorced, and moved in with his parents, who would care for him.

Don gave me a direct look as I took his hand the day we met. "I know you, don't I? You are here to help me to die." Over the years, other people have made similar comments. I do not fully understand how this process works, however it may be that our souls recognize the work we have to do together. Changes were occurring rapidly in Don's body as the disease progressed. He was not afraid to die, he assured me, but he was concerned about how his family would fare without him. Since the divorce, Don had been estranged from his two adolescent children, and he wanted desperately to reconnect with them. At his request the Hospice social worker and chaplain arranged a meeting. It was an emotional time for everyone, as the family worked through their misunderstandings and feelings of loss. At the end of the day, Don looked radiant. The last day I saw him, he could no longer stand alone. Don died within twenty-four hours after that, with his family at his side.

Dying people have what is called "Nearing Death Awareness." They know when death is near, and sometimes, but not always, can predict it to the day. Rather than be upset about this, most are quietly resigned and at peace. Most of us would agree that they are not afraid of death, but they are afraid of the dying process. They want to be in control, and they want their symptoms such as pain, nausea, or anxiety to be managed well. At times, family members tell us they do not want their loved ones to become addicted to "hard drugs." However, nothing will drain energy faster than living with pain, or nausea, or anxiety. Managing pain is both an art and a science. Share concerns with your physician and your nurses. Finally, as difficult as it may be, giving the dying person permission to leave, that you will be all right although you will miss him or her terribly, can be transformative. We have all heard stories of a family camped out in the Intensive Care room for days, never leaving the building. The moment they dash home to take a quick shower and hurry back to the patient, they find the person has slipped away quietly while they were gone. Patients often want to protect their loved ones, and hang on to life. Reassure them that you will all go on, even if you do not feel like it at the time.

THOUGHTS...

Don's story illustrates what most of us would agree, is the worst case scenario. The grace with which Don lived in the last days of his life inspires me to live in the moment, and to realize that now is the right time to have affairs in order. Make your wishes known—my cat goes to this family, I want to be as free of pain as possible (even if it means I am knocked out,) etc. Having all of this in order will prevent your loved ones from the pressure of guessing what you would have wanted.

❦

CHAPTER 3 Wally's Story

Do not stand at my grave and weep.
I am not there. I do not sleep.

I am a thousand winds that blow.
I am the diamond glint of snow.

I am the sunlight on ripened grain.
I am the gentle autumn rain.

When you wake in the morning hush
I am the swift, uplifting rush
Of quiet birds incircling flight.
I am the soft starlight at night.

Do not stand at my grave
And weep.
I am not there. I do not sleep.

Joyce Fossen

Wally was 100 percent Norwegian with a bristly white crew cut and eyes that were the vivid, deep blue of Lake Superior. "I'm from strong stock" he told me when we met. "It's tough to keep a guy like me down for long." Wally had been battling colon cancer for the past year. His wife had died five years earlier of bone cancer. It was not supposed to turn out like this, after raising six children on the family farm. I met Wally in May, the time of year when the earth is bursting with the promise of new life. Because of his condition, Wally experienced one bowel obstruction after another, frequently requiring surgery to release the obstructions. This prevented Wally from returning home, and going home was his fervent desire. "I just want to sit on my tractor in the sun one more time," he told us. Brompton's Elixir was a new cocktail for pain control that had originated in England. Open to try anything, Wally swallowed his first dose in one quick gulp. "Whee!" he crowed. "That's good stuff!"

Wally had no appetite, and despite the favorite foods his kids brought to tempt him to eat, he was unable to do so, and was getting weaker. Families often feel distraught when their loved ones don't have the desire to eat or drink. However, this is the body's mechanism to protect itself as it begins to shut down. Eating and drinking even small amounts would cause discomfort.

Finally it was decided that the trip home would be made with one of Wally's sons accompanying him.

Wally was radiant when he returned to the hospital after having been absent only two days. It was evident that a shift had occurred, and despite his smiles and hugs, he was somehow removed from the rest of us. Wally appeared to be at peace, and ready to make the transition to a new world.

THOUGHTS...

Strong stock indeed. Wally was a radiant individual who faced the unknown with faith that he would have whatever he needed to get through. He didn't ask for much...just a trip home to take stock of his life.

CHAPTER 4 John's Story

Earth mother, star mother,
You who are called by
A thousand names,
May we all remember
We are cells in your body
And dance together.
You are the grain
And the loaf
That sustains us each day,
As you are patient
With our struggles to learn
So shall we be patient
With ourselves and each other.
We are radiant light
And sacred dark
-the balance-
You are the embrace that heartens
And the freedom beyond fear.
Within you we are born
We grow, live, and die—
You bring us around the circle
To rebirth, within us you dance
Forever.

Starhawk

John was an aficionado of Minnesota sports. Walking into his home was like walking into another world. His living room consisted of an easy chair facing three television screens with score cards, remote controls, pencils and a phone sitting on a coffee table. Memorabilia (pennants, pins, cards, and anything else you could think of) going back twenty to thirty years adorned his home. This was John's castle.

John was a gentleman of sixty years of age who never married. All of his caregivers wondered how it could be that no one ever snatched him up? "Well," he told me, "if I was ready, the other person wasn't, and vice versa. It just never happened."

Just as passionate as the cross country trucks he sold, John told us exactly why they were "the Cadillac of trucks." He also wanted to get to know each of his caregivers. What were we reading, what stirred our souls, what mattered most to us in life? We all felt blessed to work with this amazing individual.

Lymphoma was the disease that John was being treated for. He told me that the treatments were not effective, and Hospice was suggested for him. John's sister and niece came to visit from the East coast. It was easy to see that they were all related—they shared an essence of goodness and an ability to quickly connect to people. As I prepared to go home one Friday evening, I got a bear hug at the door. I was scheduled to see John first thing in the morning to dress his wounds. "Drive safe- see you in the morning," he said. It was a frigid early morning when I drove to John's home. As I pulled off the freeway to the stop sign, I felt as if I had hit an energetic brick wall, and I wondered what the significance of that was. Reaching John's home, I saw both daily newspapers on his steps. I knew that if John was up and about, the first thing he would do was to retrieve the papers to peruse the sports pages. No lights were on in the home, and I became concerned. Unable to get in the door, paramedics were called. We found John on his bed, with his hands folded over his chest, looking as peaceful and innocent as a child.

THOUGHTS...

People come into our lives briefly at times, and leave a large imprint on our souls. John was one of those people. One of the gifts I learned from him was how to let go, and to live in the moment. We live our lives with the illusion that we are in control, but nothing is further from the truth.

PART II: LOVED ONES RALLY

CHAPTER 5 Mark's Story

Had you been old I might be reconciled
To see you gathered to the silent wild,
Were your days darkened, weary, shattered, told,
Had life with disillusions been defiled,
And grief poured on your head its molten gold
Had you been old-
But you were young: your faith a fire unshaken
Your bright hair tossed with the wind, your breath
swift taken,
With dear delight of earth, with arms out flung taken
To joy. Just then, just then to be forsaken
Of breath! To leave the melody unsung,
When you were young!

Elizabeth Hollister Frost

Mark was a patient on the cancer ward in a large hospital for several weeks before I met him. His lymphoma had been in remission for a few years when it returned with a vengeance. "Miracles occur on this floor with regularity," he told me the first time we met. New chemotherapy, in addition to stem cell replacement therapy, had provided a cure for many patients. But the challenge was to survive the chemo. Knowing this, Mark requested energy work to give him a boost.

Pushing his intravenous pole and visibly short of breath, Mark was waiting to be transported to have an MRI (Magnetic Resonance Imaging) of his lungs when we met. Together we decided to see how much energy work we could get in before he had to leave for the test. When I placed one hand on his chest and one on his back, Mark began to tremble, and tears rolled down his face. He had no fight left in him, he told me, and he feared what would become of his wife and three young daughters if he was unable to survive. We had forty-five minutes together, which is the usual amount of time (or longer) I spend doing energy work. The next morning, Mark told his family, "I'm back and I'm ready to fight!"

A week later was a different story, however. The chemotherapy had taken its toll, and Mark was flattened. "There are six faces that I need to see," he told me as I walked in one morning. "And yours has become one of those faces." We began our work together, and soon the emotional dam broke. I held him as the tears fell, until once again, he was at peace. "No matter what happens, it's all been worth it. I have my family back. My girls are communicating and supporting each other. I know they will be okay."

Two days later, I found Mark in the Intensive Care Unit. "I almost let myself go yesterday when the crisis hit," he told me. Despite the Herculean efforts of the physicians and staff, Mark's condition continued to deteriorate. Finally, he was allowed to go home with Hospice care. I saw him the evening before he died, and I felt grateful to have one more session of energy work with him as he prepared for his final journey. Family and friends stood around the bed as we watched Mark become less restless and his respiration slower. All through the night, his large, extended family and friends camped out in his home and kept a vigil. Mark seemed to be aware that they were there, and appeared to be at peace. He died early the next morning. He was fifty-three, the same age as his father, who died thirty years and one day previously.

THOUGHTS...

In death as in life, Mark emerged victorious. Despite all that he endured during the last weeks in the hospital, he moved mountains. He was not a man who was accustomed to baring his soul, but all of that changed. Because he was able to communicate in a new way with his wife and young daughters, they began to be open to each other, offering the support they so desperately needed. His is truly an inspirational story. Mark validated for me that it is never too late to create new paradigms of communicating and being.

CHAPTER 6 Gabriel's Story

Absolutely Clear

Don't send your loneliness
So quickly
Let it cut more deep.
Let it ferment and season you
As few human
Or even divine ingredients can.
Something missing in my heart tonight
Has made my eyes so soft,
My voice
So tender,
My need of God
Absolutely
Clear.

Hafiz

In the late 1980s, the AIDS epidemic was rampant and young men and women were dropping like flies. In south Minneapolis, a private home was converted into a Hospice for young men with AIDS. Brother Martin, a Franciscan monk, operated the home with great love. Every day many volunteers came to assist. A pot of homemade soup always on the stove and fresh bread baking in the oven. I was introduced as a volunteer to a young man named Gabriel, who looked like a cherub with his curly blond hair, blue eyes, and dimples. As a result of the AIDS virus and diabetes, Gabriel became blind. We spent each Saturday together. Gabriel was quickly losing weight, and my job was to try to encourage him to eat, then bathe him in the tub, and finally, just hang out. Gabriel loved to talk. We discovered that we shared many of the same interests: music, art, poetry, children, cooking, and animals. As we sat in the dining room, I would hold a spoonful of soup or homemade bread, waiting for Gabriel to stop talking long enough to slip it into his mouth.

Brother Martin passed through the dining room at one time, and asked, "Gabriel? Is your mouth full?"

"Why no, Brother, it isn't," Gabriel replied with a smile.

Brother Martin spooned the soup into Gabriel's mouth, saying, "Now it is! Keep it that way!"

After lunch was, as Gabriel called it, "The treat of the week," a tub bath. This was a time when Gabriel expounded on his favorite topics, how wonderful it felt to have his hair shampooed, the sensuality of water, how he loved the endless variety of colors, and of course, food. Because he was a diabetic, Gabriel was not allowed to have the rich sauces and French cuisine that he had so loved to prepare. Still, he delighted in talking about them—and all types of foods. We found we shared another interest: music. At times we would hum or sing snippets of piano music we used to play, or arias that we both loved. Divas we were not. But we had a lot of fun.

Gabriel grew up in rural Minnesota. An art teacher in primary education, he had worked as long as he could until he became too weak to continue. To his delight, the children sent him boxes of carefully made get well cards. Not long after receiving them, Gabriel's vision failed, and he told us how grateful he was to be able to remember how those cards looked. Many were painted with beautiful yellow roses, which were Gabriel's favorite flower.

One day I received a call from Brother Martin "Gabriel is changing fast, and I do not know if he will be here on Saturday. I know Gabriel wants to see you," he said.

I quickly drove to Brother Martin's home, yellow roses in hand. In Gabriel's room, a candle was burning, soft music was playing, and it appeared that he had slipped into a coma. As I placed the roses on his bedside, to my surprise, Gabriel turned his face to me, and said "Kate? I knew you would come. I took his hand and told Gabriel that I loved him and would never forget him. Then next morning Martin called to let me now Gabriel died peacefully in his sleep. For many years after that, I joined the fundraiser for AIDS care and walked in honor of Gabriel. Whenever I hear a beautiful aria, or make homemade soup or bread, I am reminded of him.

What can you do if your loved one is in a coma when you arrive? Arnold Mindell tells us in "Coma", that great work is being done at this sacred time, and communication is very important. Place your hand on the persons chest, place your face close to theirs, and match your respirations to theirs. If any small moans or sounds are made, softly mimic them and or speak very softly into their ear. Using a very light touch may be helpful as well. Energetically, this communicates to the patient that you are there with them, offering support. It may be a time of coming to terms with their lives, or of gaining a final understanding of their purpose on this earth. It is precious, sacred time. There have even been instances where the patient awakened to make a few necessary statements before feeling free to move on.

THOUGHTS...

Sometimes the only thing we can offer someone who is dying is to be there. A hand to hold, or stories to be listened to validate the beauty and meaning their life. Gabriel taught me that no matter what the circumstances, the ability to savor and cherish life need not be diminished.

CHAPTER 7 Bonnie's Story

Roses shine in the clay

Beside your tomb.
Be aware, earth,

Who sleeps inside of you!

Rumi

On a sleepy morning in June, a family of five was preparing for a long anticipated journey out west. Finally the lists were all crossed off, the house locked up tight, and the van rolled down the driveway. "We're off!!" exclaimed Brian, the father of the bunch, to cheers and laughter.

The family never made it out of town that day. When Bonnie experienced sharp pain in her back, the family pulled into the emergency room of a large inner-city hospital. Bonnie was admitted, and tests were run. The van stayed packed overnight, in hopes that in the morning the family would be able to resume the journey. The next day Bonnie and Brian faced the news that at the age of forty-two, Bonnie had renal (kidney) cancer, and at most, had about one year to live.

What sounds do dreams make when they shatter? The family returned home, and Bonnie began aggressive rounds of chemotherapy. After just six months of treatment with no results, it was decided that it was time for Hospice.

Brian was a bear of a man, "a hugger" and a source of strength and comfort to the entire family. He and Bonnie were high school sweethearts who shared a deep faith, and were raising three young children.

Bonnie experienced pain and nausea, which stubbornly did not respond well to medication. However, energy medicine brought blessed relief. "It's gone!" Bonnie reported to us that her symptoms were relieved for three days after receiving a treatment. At the end of each session, Bonnie would take my hands in hers and say, "Please wait." We sat with our eyes closed until Bonnie released my hands. When I asked her what happened during those moments, she replied, "I am praying for you."

Bonnie asked to be discharged from the hospital on the day she died. She did not want her children to be traumatized by witnessing their mother die at home, so she asked her mother to take her to her home instead. Bonnie's mother had battled anxiety all of her life, but she stepped up to the plate. "I brought her into this world, and I can help her to leave it, too." Bonnie died within hours of being transferred to her mother's home—with her family surrounding her.

THOUGHTS...

A young wife and mother, Bonnie left the world far too soon. Words lose something in translation, in describing the bright being that Bonnie was. From the first time I met her, I felt I was in the presence of some-one very special. Bonnie was a rock for everyone who loved her, and radiated strength, faith, and courage. She seemed to have one foot in this world, and one in the next.

PART III: EASING THE WAY TO THE VEIL AND BEYOND

CHAPTER 8 Katia's Story

BLESS OUR COURAGE
In the midst of life
We are in death.
The Spirit of our beloved sister
Dwells in our hearts.
We have the courage, in love,
To carry forward her memory
In the lives we now lead.
Let the best which was her,
Be renewed in strength in us.
May we now give to others the love
That we can no longer give to her,
For the lives we lead now are
Her honor and her memorial.
She would bless our courage.
May we have peace.
She would wish it so.
So let it be.
Author unknown

A tall, willowy, redhead with dramatic features and a sparkling wit, Katia had no fear of death. After battling ovarian cancer for three years, she told me that she was tired. Although she lived alone, when the time came that she needed more help, her cousins took turns staying with her. I told them how impressed I was with their dedication. "There's a reason for that," they smiled and told me. Years earlier Katia's mother, Anne, set the standard for the rest of the family. She was the healer/caregiver who dropped what she was doing, leaving her two young daughters in the care of their father, when other family members needed help. Whenever someone gave birth, became ill, or had surgery, Anne stayed with them until they were back on their feet. I thought about what a sacrifice that must have been, and what a legacy she left behind.

Katia had experienced energy work previously, and was eager to begin. As soon as we started our session, she told me that she saw a large, clear dome covering both of us. In one corner, her favorite grandmother sat in her rocking chair, and in another corner sat Katia's beloved cat, Wilbur (who had died several years earlier), purring loudly. After a period of time, Katia reported that Christ leaned over the dome, murmured, "This is good," and left. Katia told us she felt at peace at the end of this first session. As days went by, Katia told us that her deceased parents and sister Sophia, were frequent visitors and that she found comfort in their presence.

As Angeles Arrien tells us in "The Fourfold Way," many indigenous cultures believe that the Spirits of our Ancestors are present when we are preparing to die. Frequently patients will report that a deceased loved one visits or "is sitting right over there." This does not necessarily mean that the person is confused nor is it the result of strong medications. Finally, Katia became weaker and could only whisper. One morning she beckoned for me to come close. "I want you to know," she told me, "when I get to wherever it is I'm going to, I'll always be looking out for you." Frequently I feel Katia's unique energy with me, especially if I am upset about something I can't control. It's as if she reassures me that this is not something worth being upset about. She also encourages me to try to find humor in the situation.

Days passed, and Katia began to withdraw from her friends and family. People ask why, when the time left is so precious, can't they make the most of it rather than withdrawing? My sense is that they are doing important work before entering into a new life. Another frequent question is, why does it take so long to die? Perhaps there is unfinished business, forgiveness that needs to be requested or received, or a reconnection is necessary with someone. Perhaps one simply needs the time to take stock of one's life, and understand its purpose. It takes as long as it takes. Try to remember that survival is our strongest instinct, and our bodies are not programmed to stop functioning.

THOUGHTS...

Becoming aware of the love, support, and assistance available to us just beyond the veil requires us to let go of judgments. Our normal faculties of sight, hearing, and perception were not designed for communication with the invisible world of Spirit. We need to be sensitive to our feelings, intuition, and the slightest shift in our heart. With practice, and by suspending judgment about rationality, the process becomes easier.

CHAPTER 9 Helen's Story

Be patient toward all that is unsolved in your heart
and try to love the questions themselves-like locked
rooms and locked manuals that are written in a very
foreign tongue...and the point is to live everything.
Live the questions now, perhaps you will then, grad-
ually, without noticing it, live along some
day into the answer.

Rilke

A vivacious, green eyed blond, it seemed a particularly cruel twist of fate that ALS (Amyotrophic Lateral Sclerosis or Lou Geri's Disease), would claim Helen at the age of sixty. "To know Helen is to love Helen," as one of her caregivers aptly stated. Always more focused on others than on herself, she had legions of friends. With undeniable spirit and flair, she taught us how to live life to the fullest while dealing with a terminal disease. Each morning her beloved husband, Dale, would bathe and dress her, carefully apply makeup, and finally style her hair. On warm, sunny days he would lift her, wearing Jackie-O sunglasses and a long scarf to flow in the wind, into their BMW convertible for a spin around the lake where they lived, to visit friends.

A pragmatic woman, Helen was never interested in alternative therapies. She agreed to explore one session of energy work, however, with her healthy skepticism intact. Resting on the bed, she closed her eyes as we began, then shook her head. "Amazing," she kept repeating. "This is just amazing." She began to describe the vision that she saw. Sitting in a room with a hole in the roof, and an arched doorway, was her maternal grandfather, who died prior to Helen's birth. Helen recognized him, she told us, from a photo. Also present was Mary, a dear friend who died many years earlier. During this session, Helen was given a glimpse of what she called "the big picture." She told us that she was no longer afraid to die. During subsequent sessions, Helen's mother, who was alive and well at the age of 93, appeared in the room as a young girl with her father, dressed in the fashion of the day, with a bow in her hair.

Helen extended an invitation to her family and close friends to rest beside her on her bed one by one during our sessions. She continued to give a verbal running account of everything that she saw. Her grandfather was a faithful visitor to "the room in between," as we began to call it. One day, however, no one appeared in the room. Moments passed, as tears rolled down her cheeks and Helen said she felt abandoned and devastated. Then, inexplicably, she did not speak for several moments. Deep peace settled over me like a mantle, and permeated to the core of my being. Helen spoke, "Kate did you feel that? The peace?" She then described that a brilliant white light emerged from the arched doorway, bringing with it soul abiding deep peace.

Anger is a powerful emotion that needs to be dealt with during the dying process, and Helen was not exempt from it. "I want a miracle and I want it right now!" she proclaimed during one session. Speaking to Christ Helen said "You raised Lazarus from the dead; I know you can do it. Come on, give it to me!" After waiting for a few moments, she sadly shook her head. "No miracles for Helen," she murmured. "They are preparing a place for me." Expressing the grief and loss that her old life was over, Helen did not stay immersed in anger for long. She found the courage to move on.

As the disease progressed, it became more difficult for Helen to speak and swallow. "I don't want to live if I can't talk," she told us. At times unable to enunciate a word, with great patience she would spell it out, beaming a radiant smile as we understood her. Her condition began to take a toll on her family, as well. "It's so hard to see the sad faces of my loved ones."

Once again during our session, no one appeared to be in the room in between. "I want to come home," she implored. "I have fought the good fight. I am begging to come home." Christ appeared through the arched doorway, carrying a small lamb in His arms. "Come to me all you who are burdened, and I will give you rest" Then, "Let peace, like a river, flow through your veins", and then he was gone.

Although Ludwig, Helen's Grandfather, and Mary, Helen's dear friend, frequently invited Helen to visit them in the room where they resided, she felt reluctant to do so. She told us she was afraid she might not be able to come back. However, not much later, with her daughter Jenna beside her on the bed she found herself in the room, and she was not paralyzed. She could walk! Helen and Ludwig embraced for the first time,. Ludwig told Helen "I have been with you since the moment you were born." Christ then appeared and motioned for Helen to open the door under the arch. Helen began to tremble on the bed and did not speak for a few moments. She told us that a magnificent opaline stairway climbing into the heavens was visible in the distance, and that the peace and beauty of that world were beyond words. Interestingly enough, this was one of the few visions that Helen had, that I was allowed to see.

As the days passed, it became obvious to all who loved her that Helen's time on earth was drawing to a close. During one of our last sessions, Helen again described that saw herself standing in the room in between, this time with myself standing next to her, holding her hand. As she told us we both walked over to where Christ was standing, and He said to her: "Good and faithful servant, the gates of heaven are open to you. We will wrap our arms around you and carry you home." "I want Kate to come with me," she implored. Although I did not see the vision or hear the words except when Helen repeated them to us, I began to get a little concerned. Did I sign up for this? Christ answered Helen that I could not come with her, that my work was unfinished. I could accompany her to the gates of heaven, but not through them. Helen described each of her visions in great detail. At times I had a sense of Helen's vision was, but usually I did not see what she did. The last picture she shared was of both of us ascending the beautiful white staircase, hand in hand.

THOUGHTS...

Every one of us can choose to become a vessel or conduit for Spirit to work through. Helen's stories seemed to bolster the faith of everyone who heard them. Part of Helen's legacy is to remind us of the help and love available just beyond the veil of this existence. Helen slipped into a coma shortly before she died. According to her family, she broke into a huge "toothy" grin and appeared to be talking to someone. Early the next morning, she died peacefully in her sleep with her family at her bedside.

Helen showed us all to live fully in the moment with a terminal disease. She exuded grace, warmth, and courage to everyone she met. She helped her family by planning her funeral, and even went shopping with Dale to buy confirmation gifts for her grandchildren in the years to come. Helen did not bury her anger, rather she showed us how to work through it. Everyone who met Helen felt like a better person after spending time with her.

CHAPTER 10 Tanya's Story

To live in this world
You must be able to do three things:
To love what is mortal,
To hold it against your bones knowing
Your own life depends upon it
And, when the time comes to let it go,
To let it go.

Mary Oliver

Tanya was a radiant forty-two year old woman with rapidly advancing ALS, Amyotrophic Lateral Sclerosis, when I met her. Cared for by her soul mate and loving husband, Jeff, they wanted to try anything they could to bring themselves peace. Because Tanya was on a Bi-pap, or partial respirator, it took a great effort for her to talk, swallow, and cough. She closed her eyes as we began the energy work. Almost immediately, she broke into a huge grin, began to laugh, and then cry, nodding "yes." Jeff and I exchanged bewildered glances, not knowing what she was experiencing. This happened several times in the course of an hour. Afterward, both Jeff and Tanya appeared to be at peace and slumbering. I tiptoed out of the home.

The next week Tanya was feeling a bit better and was eager to share her experience with Jeff and me. A Native American Indian had appeared who had white hair, and held in his outstretched arms a pair of suede beaded boots, lined in rabbit fur. He told her these would be the boots that would take her to the other side. "He told me I have come full circle in this life," Tanya beamed to us. "He said, and now I know, that everything will be all right, for all of us," she said, looking at Jeff. "How come I never was aware of this beautiful other world?" she asked. She gained the belief and understanding that her purpose on the other side would be to emanate love, and that she could be a more powerful force for the good from this place.

As days passed, I learned that Tanya and Jeff had known each other many years earlier, while both were stationed in Europe. Life being life, their wonderful relationship ended, with each of them returning home to marry another and have children. Nearly eight years before I met them they had found each other, married, and lived "in bliss," until ALS came into the picture.

Tanya's physicians told them that this was one of the most aggressive cases of ALS that they had encountered. As the disease quickly progressed, we all realized that Tanya's days were numbered. Tanya asked Jeff to keep a promise to her: if she could not take it any longer and knew it was time to go, that he would help her. He would remove the respirator, keep her comfortable with medications, but if, for even one second she changed her mind, he would reconnect the respirator. She awakened one day to tell her husband, "This is the day!" I was nonetheless shocked to get the call that she had peacefully died in her sleep–with Jeff's arms around her. He shared with me their final conversations. At no time did she feel uncomfortable, breathless, anxious, or in pain. At first she saw a white dove. Then, Jeff told me, a white path appeared before her, which she was standing on. Not much later, Tanya said, angels appeared. "They're huge, and have big wings!" Finally, Tanya saw her uncle, Bill, who had died two weeks earlier. Moments later she slipped quietly away.

When I heard the news, I felt devastated that this bright being had to leave so soon, and I talked aloud to her as I drove to visit my dad on his farm. Suddenly I saw a vision of Tanya, standing before me in a long suede dress with fringe and wearing her beautiful traveling boots. "Don't be sad," she told me. Everything is going to be OK, and I will be your helper." One morning a few months later, before I was fully awake and had opened my eyes, I felt Tanya's presence and heard her voice, whispering, "Everything will be all right." I remember feeling her essence and a feeling of deep peace...

THOUGHTS...

It is a privilege and an honor to do this work, and it is as challenging as it is rewarding. When working with younger people who have so much to offer, I can't help but ask why and feel deep grief. There are no answers. There never were any answers and that itself is the answer. I feel deeply grateful to have known each one of my clients, and to have been present with them during such an intimate time of need, and unknowing. I feel their individual essence with me frequently; that is a large part of what gets me through and enables me to heal.

CHAPTER 11 Ann's Story

"Who Dies?"

It is because you believe that you are born that you
fear death.
Who is it that was born?
Who is it that dies?
Look within.
What was your face before you were born?
Who you are, in reality, was never born and never
dies.
Let go of who you think you are and become who you
have always been.

Steven Levine

Ann lived with her sisters, Rose and Hannah where they were raised with their three brothers. Their parents were immigrants and "clannish", as Ann described them. "We didn't have coffee or meals with other folks. We minded our own business." None of the siblings ever married. The three sisters spent their entire lives working for a national company and saving for trips they planned to take once they reached retirement. They collected travel brochures and talked about looking up distant relatives in the old country. Ann had been doctoring for a stubborn cough for over a year. The antibiotics and cough medicine did not offer much relief. Rising early one morning, Hannah thought "How odd. I don't hear Ann getting ready, and we still have lunches to make." She entered Anne's room to find her still in bed, crying. "I can't move my legs!" In the hospital a chest x-ray showed a tumor in her lung that also invaded her spine. Chemo therapy and radiation were tried with little success. Ann was sent home with Hospice Care. The sisters were stricken and perplexed. They never smoked nor drank, lived only clean lives, and did not comprehend how this could happen to Ann. It seemed that their dreams vanished into thin air.

Once Ann's cares were completed in the morning, she enjoyed being wheeled out to spend some time in the garden. The rich Connecticut soil grew heirloom tomatoes and dinner plate sized dahlias. One afternoon Ann's physician made a house call. Ann was weaker and no longer able to get out of bed. As we walked him to the door, we asked how much time Ann had left. He did not look at us as he said, "Ann will just fall off of a cliff. It will happen quickly."

One morning I arrived and Ann had a far away, peaceful look on her face. "Ma came to visit me. I used to sleep upstairs but this was Ma's room, where she died. I guess I'll die here, too. Ma told me everything will be all right, there is no reason to be afraid." Ann was unusually quiet for the rest of the day. She seemed to be most content to sit without talking, holding hands. Late that night the phone rang, and Hannah sounded distressed. Ann lost consciousness and her breathing was erratic. We stayed at Ann's side until with one last breath, she was gone.

THOUGHTS

Anne's legacy seems to be live fully today-don't wait for your dreams to come true years down the line. Don't just wait for special occasions, use the good china! Live each moment to the fullest experiencing the joy, hope sadness of life and let go of any negativity. This moment in time is all that we have.

PART IV: WILLINGNESS TO BE OPEN

CHAPTER 12 Luke's Story

Oh, for so short a while
Have you loaned us to each other.
Because we take form in your act of drawing us
And we breathe in you singing us.
But only for a short while
Have you loaned us to each other.
Because even a drawing cut in
Crystalline obsidian fades,
And the green feathers, the crown feathers
Of the Quetzal bird lose their color,
And even sounds of the waterfall
Dies out in the dry season.
So, we too, because only for short a while
Have you loaned us to each other.

Aztec prayer to God

One stormy Friday afternoon in late spring, I was asked if I could attend to a young man, Luke, who was close to death. I was greeted at the door by his mother, Marie, a native woman. "The storms clouds came to take my son away," she told me, with tears flowing. As I entered the bedroom where her son was, I saw the body of a young man, only twenty-eight years of age. "Tell me what happened," I asked Marie and her husband. He died of cirrhosis of the liver, they told me, just as Marie's other son had two years earlier. "Drinking is the bane of my people's existence." Witnessing her grief and pain, I felt heavyhearted and wondered how parents could survive a tragedy such as this. I asked if they would like to help me to prepare their son's body before it was taken to the funeral home. They were eager to begin. We lit a candle, and I asked if there was special music Luke enjoyed. His mother produced a drumming and native chants CD. "Tell me about Luke," I asked as we began. "What was he like as a little boy?"

Marie's face softened as she remembered Luke years earlier. "He was the gentle, sensitive one. An artist. He loved to draw and carve. If someone was sad, Luke was the one to try to make you feel better."

With great tenderness we combed and braided Luke's hair, bathed his body, and anointed it with oil. The parents spoke of their wishes for Luke as we continued. "To see with the eyes of an eagle. To fly with the wind. To always feel the love that his family and friends had for him in their hearts, and to learn from the wisdom of the ancestors, whose company he now keeps." Finally we dressed him in soft clothing, and sat quietly together until they were ready to release his body. "We will take him to South Dakota, to the reservation, to rest beside his brother and grandparents. It is where he should be."

As I left that afternoon, I wished that I had had the opportunity to know Luke and his family better. I felt deeply moved to have shared in the ritual we performed for him.

THOUGHTS…

Many cultures do not believe the soul immediately leaves , but may stay around for as long as a few hours. During this time try to think and speak only positive thoughts. Connect with their spirit , tell them what is in your heart, and assure them that you will be ok. Even if we are unable to be with a loved one at the time actual time of death, our love for them may still be felt

CHAPTER 13 Energy Medicine

Before I met Steve, his nurse manager advised me, "Be on time, not five minutes too early or too late. Steve will have a list of questions for you, and when your assessment has been completed, he will walk out of the room, dismissing you. Don't take it personally." And sure enough, the visit proceeded as I had been told. However, a voice in my mind kept telling me that this man needed energy work. Feeling that I was out on a limb, I spoke up. I told him there was something else I felt I could offer to him to make him feel better. Steve said he was curious and skeptical, and decided to give it a try. He settled into his favorite recliner, and Tanya, his wife, left the room. Steve quickly fell into a slumber; his respiration slowed and he snored softly. Soon Tanya came back into the room, saying, "I could feel that energy all the way upstairs. May I sit in?" I assured her that her presence was welcome. After nearly an hour, Steve awakwened. "Well!" he exclaimed "I haven't ever experienced anything like this! Do you have a card? Do they offer this to all the Hospice patients? What is the Director's name? I'm going to give her a call!" It is good for people to keep their healthy skepticism intact. It was rewarding that Steve, who had been an executive and was used to being in control, would be open to an alternative approach.

According to the ancients, we consist of a mass of energy or consciousness that includes our physical body, our thoughts, feelings, and emotions. Energy is not good or bad, it just is. Energy is free flowing and can be molded, directed, and manipulated to produce various realities in our life. We create this reality through our intent.

In Deepok Chopra's book, "Life After Death", he describes consciousness, or energy, in this way: "Consciousness of subtle objects is the world of dreams, imagination, and inspiration in all its forms. We verify the world through intuition and feelings of subtle pressure within and without that are not viable to the five senses. As your body becomes more and more alive through the activation of your senses, sensing is what you do instead of thinking. Awareness is focused through your senses, noticing all that you sense. As your consciousness begins to move out of the brain, you leave the analytical mind behind. You begin to find the world that our ancient ancestors knew so well."

Human touch is a basic need for all of us. We know that babies who don't receive enough touch, fail to thrive. For a person who is ill or in the process of dying, energy work can be a powerful tool to relieve pain or anxiety. Always ask permission before you begin. Usually it is safe to provide gentle touch on the feet, hands, shoulders, and head. For other areas of the body, ask first. If pain is present in a certain area, ask if you can place your hands there. If a person is processing grief or loss, place one hand on the heart area and one in the back. Imagine energy flowing from one hand to the other. This can help to reduce grief and sadness. While you continue, be aware of your own thoughts and feelings, and let your intuition be your guide. Don't be afraid to ask for feedback, if that is a possibility, and share your own perceptions as well. Some people prefer silence during this process, and to share what happened later. Some people may experience visions, or voices or sounds, and most will feel very peaceful. Energy work can be provided for a few minutes, or for as long as an hour. I have been told many times that energy work is the only thing that has relieved pain, nausea, or anxiety. On a scale of one to ten with ten being the most excruciating type of pain, people regularly report that the pain recedes to a one or two. It is a great tool to add to the mix. Remember: try to let go of expectations to outcomes.

The Physicality of Death

One lovely spring Sunday, I was asked to see a thirty-four year-old man who was actively dying of a brain tumor. His wife met me at the door and said, "He is dying and in so much pain. Is there anything you can do?" I quickly explained how energy medicine could help him, as his family gathered around the bed. His respirations slowed after a few minutes, and his restlessness abated. After some time, his respirations became more shallow until he died. Did the energy alleviate his pain? It is hard to say. It seemed evident, however, that he became more peaceful and slipped away quietly.

What happens when we die? How can families be aware that death is imminent and be prepared? In the dying process, usually a few days before the death, patients may smile and tell us that their deceased loved one " sat right here, on the bed last night." More likely than not, they are not hallucinating. At this time the veil between the worlds is thin, and dying people may see and hear things that we are not able to. We know from scientists who study near death experiences that as a person loses consciousness, their hearing remains. It is never too late to tell someone that you love them, and that you will be all right. Respirations may become irregular, with long spaces in between called Cheynne Stokes. Mucous may collect in the throat and cause a slight gurgling sound known as the "death rattle." As distressing as this may be to hear, it does not necessarily mean that the person is in great discomfort. It is simply air flowing over the vocal chords As blood in the body moves to vital organs, feet and lower legs may turn a mottled or bluish color. The Dali Lama tells us in his book on Death and Dying that he believes the soul does not immediately leave the body and may linger for as long as two hours. It may be helpful to stay with the body for a period of time after the death.

A beautiful ritual that can be performed prior to or directly after a death is the blessing of the body. I encourage family members to assist if they want to. We light a candle, and if there is music that the deceased enjoyed, we play it. A drop of rose or lavender oil may be added to a basin of water. The story that follows is an illustration of how one family did a blessing of the body for their father.

David and his wife raised five lovely daughters. They described him as a very hands-on kind of a dad who read the Sunday funnies with the girls on his lap He attended all their games, and enjoyed roughhousing with the girls. The family lived in a two-bedroom rambler with only one bathroom upstairs. David hooked up a shower stall in the basement and kept the cobwebs intact so the girls would not be tempted to take it over.

Early one morning I was told that David had died, and his daughters had requested a visit to the home. When I arrived, the women told me they kept a vigil all night with their father. They played his favorite bluegrass and rock and roll music, sharing memories and tears. They were happy to perform the blessing of the body. The following blessing is from Starhawk:

I bless your hair that the wind has played with.

I bless your brow, your thoughts.

I bless your eyes that have looked on us with love.

I bless your ears that have listened to your voices.

I bless your nostrils gateway of breath.

I bless your lips that have spoken truth.

I bless your neck and throat; we will remember your voice.

I bless your neck and shoulders that have born burdens with strength.

I bless your arms that have embraced us.

I bless your hands that have shaped wonders.

I bless your breasts that have nurtured us formed in strength and beauty.

I bless your ribs and lungs that sustained your life.

I bless your solar plexus, seat of power.

I bless your belly, sacred storehouse of the body.

I bless your womb that gave life that bled with the moon.

I bless your hips, the Child's first cradle, strong support.

I bless your thighs, strong boundaries.

I bless your knees that knelt at the sacred altars.
I bless your legs that carried you.
I bless your feet that walked your own path through
life.

CHAPTER 14 Getting Through it

A New Way of Thinking

I am letting you go and wishing you well. I am going to
survive and be strong.
I am going to make a new life for myself.
It takes courage to grieve.
It takes courage to feel our pain and face the
unfamiliar.
It also takes courage to grieve in a society
That mistakenly values restraint,
Where we risk the rejection of others
By being open, or different.

Christine Longaker, 1997

Grief is the emotion we feel as a result of opening our hearts and souls to loving a person, place, animal, or thing. It is for a time a painful process that eventually heals and is woven into the tapestry of our lives. The pain recedes, but a scar may remain. Elizabeth Kubler-Ross listed five stages of grief: denial, anger, bargaining, depression, and acceptance. We know that one does not go through the five stages consecutively. Grief is an individual process, and if it is not dealt with, it will not just disappear. Unresolved grief can be manifested in physical symptoms such as hypertension, anxiety, stroke, heart attack, to name a few. If you have concerns about someone who has had a loss, share your feelings and empathize about how difficult life must be when nothing is the same anymore. Rusty Berkus writes in her beautifully illustrated book "To Heal Again" remember that there is no right way or wrong way to grieve; there is just your way. It takes as long as it takes. During this time, it is ever so important to be gentle, loving, and kind with yourself. There is a cycle to everything, and you will emerge from the darkness into the light. George Bonnano, a psychologist at the Columbia Teaching College, found that bereaved individuals who naturally avoid emotion should not be forced to confront their grief. Even three years later such people show no trauma as a result of suppressing it, he reported. Christine Longaker reminds us that most of us are aware of our fear of death. However, we may have an even deeper fear of grief. We equate grieving with dying, hopelessness and helplessness. We don't trust that going through bereavement, grief and loss, means that we will come out the other side. Thus we resist grieving as though it were the worst thing that could happen to us. Each change requires a new level of grieving and letting go.

What about unresolved grief? We have all heard of people who die from a broken heart after a loss. Perhaps these individuals never faced their losses, or worked through their emotions. Robert Niemayer, professor of psychology at the University of Memphis and editor of the Scientific Journal of Death Studies, gives these guidelines: "If a month down the road the person has intrusive thoughts about the deceased or recurrent images of how the person died, feelings of purposelessness or that the world cannot be trusted are indicators that something needs to be addressed." On the other hand, a report on "Bereavement and Grief Research" prepared by the Center for the Advancement of Health concludes that a growing body of evidence indicates that intervention with adults who are not experiencing complicated grief cannot be regarded as beneficial in terms of diminishing grief-related symptoms.

I once had the honor of co-facilitating a grief and loss support group for the elderly. One of our guidelines was for individuals to wait until four months passed before joining the group. We met once a week for three months at a time. Although I felt seasoned in dealing with grief, I was not prepared for the extent of losses these amazing individuals had experienced. Their resiliency and faith in the goodness of life, and their desire to heal and live full lives once again had a great impact on me. Some were more stoic than others, and although they were happy to be in the group, they did not wish to speak much about their losses.

Losing a loved one is one of the biggest losses we may ever face. We cannot outrun this emotion. There is no way around it. Grief takes as long as it takes. There is a cycle to grief, and you will emerge from the darkness into the light. To be with our grief allows our souls to breathe.

Christina Feldman tells us in "Stories of the Spirit, Stories of the Heart""Anything that can be lost was never truly ours, anything that we cling to only imprisons us.. We are never the owners, the possessors of the things in our lives. Even our children are here with us for a time. We live in relationship to them either skillfully and wisely or graspingly and unwisely. Even our bodies do not belong to us. They are gifts which will change and eventually need to be released in their own way. Their changing cycles reflect the very nature of the world. When we learn to be truly present, we discover that what we deeply seek has always been with us."

Indigenous and other cultures weave ritual into the daily tapestry of their lives. Children learn from an early age that death is a part of life not to be feared, and the spirits of their ancestors live among them. We can incorporate ritual into our lives very simply. The act of lighting a candle and invoking an intention or prayer is a ritual. Ritual is intensely personal and is collaboration between us and the spirit world. It can be multilayered with lots of props (such as celebrated in a Catholic Mass, or a May Day ritual celebrating spring). Ritual tells us that an event has occurred that has changed our lives. It also is a beautiful vehicle to connect with the world of Spirit-whether asking for help or giving thanks. In our daily lives, we can seek strength and assistance from the world of Spirit. Ritual tells us our lives have been irrevocably changed, and this act begins to start to put the pieces back together. Even after the funeral, small, personal rituals can have a powerful impact in healing our grief. If there are words that were left unsaid, create an altar or space in your home and sit before it. Express what is in your heart, and know that you will be heard. When we need support, we usually call upon our inner circle of friends. Consider opening that circle to include those who are beyond the veil. Whether you call upon someone on this plane of existence or beyond, trust that you will be heard.

Out beyond ideas of wrongdoing and right doing,

there's a field-I'll meet you there.

Rumi

We are taught to run from our brokenness. I learned from reading Julia Cameron's manual, The *Artist's Way* that "Anger is a powerful emotion to be dealt with. Anger is meant to be respected. Why? Because anger is a MAP. Anger shows us what our boundaries are and where we want to go. It lets us know when we haven't liked it. Anger points the way." Like grief, anger won't just go away, and will wreak havoc in our bodies if left unattended. We may be surprised with the ferocity of it once we allow it to have its own voice. Ways to deal with it are to voice your anger while scrubbing the floor, walking the dog, in the shower, journaling. Pay attention to the relief you will feel which may be in small increments at first, and notice how this process opens your heart. You will know you have made progress when you feel lighter.

It is never too late to bridge the gulf of misunderstanding. "There are two causes for misunderstanding. One is not saying what you mean, and the other is not doing what you say." It takes courage to show up, and be present. Simply stating that "I am sorry we lost all of this time. Whatever happened in the past doesn't matter anymore." Or, "I did not know how to bridge this gap," are ways to begin.

COMPASSION

Christina Feldman and Jack Kornfield give a beautiful description of compassion: Compassion is that singular quality of heart that has the power to transform resentment into forgiveness, anger into loving kindness. It is the most precious quality of our being that allows us to extend warmth, sensitivity and openness to the world around us and to ourselves, rather than be burdened by prejudice, hostility, and resentment.

We have all been in situations where we feel we have been mistreated. Perhaps you were right, and it would be easy to place blame and harbor resentments. What if you have unresolved issues with someone who is dying? It doesn't matter if the other person is present, willing to communicate with us ,forgive us or be forgiven. What matters is our intention to heal and release old baggage. Sometimes acting "as if" is the first step that we need to take. Visualize the other person sitting across from you, in an open and receptive state of being. Communicate in words or thoughts without the emotional impact, or feelings of right or wrongdoing. Think of what the issue was and your intention to release it. You are operating from your Highest Self and communicating to that part of the other person. "Blessing" Gregg Braden tells us, is the ancient secret that releases us from life's hurt long enough to replace it with another feeling. When we bless the people or things that have hurt us, we are temporarily suspending the cycle of pain. It doesn't matter if this lasts a nanosecond or an entire day. During the blessing a doorway opens for us to begin our healing and move on with life." Henri Nouwen offers this map to peace:

"As long as we do not forgive those who have wounded us, we carry them with us, or worse, pull them along as a heavy load…The great temptation is to cling in anger to our enemies and then define ourselves as being offended and wounded by them. Forgiveness, therefore, liberates not only the other, but us. It is the way to freedom."

Carl Jung tells us "Meaning makes a great many things endurable- perhaps everything" If we are unable to forgive ourselves or others we remain cemented to the past and there is no closure. Finally, look into your own heart to see if anything else needs to be addressed. Feel the space that has been opened there as a result of your taking this action. Say goodbye, and wish the other person well.

SPIRIT
Gregg Braden shares what ancient traditions have always known and what quantum physics has now

proven to us: that there is something out there, a web, a force, a connectedness, which he describes as the Divine Matrix. "It is the great net that links us with one another, our world, and a greater power." DNA in our bodies gives us access to the energy that connects to our universe, and emotion is the key to communicating with the field. Father Ed Hays talks about the world that is just beyond the veil

"Parents, teachers, and those who have loved you in life, love you beyond the grave. They, more than earthly teachers, desire that you reach your birthright destination and are eager to assist you. They go wherever love draws them. Do not be afraid to call on them for assistance. Since your normal sense organs are not designed for such communication, you must be sensitive for the slightest touch of the heart, to intuition, feelings, and even apprehensions that are beyond the merely rational. Your inner eyes and ears as well as your heart must be open."

John Dryden, a seventeenth century poet reflects:

Our souls sit close and silently within
And their own webs from their own sense is such
That spider-like, we feel the tenderest touch.

Hospice patients have told me through the years that they would always be watching out for me, and I have learned to be closely attuned to this. One winter day I felt the sense that something was amiss with one of my patients. I decided to call to find out if they were all right. The son answered and said indeed, it had been an emotional day as their father declined during the night.

Could I stop out? I was grateful to be present for this family in a time of need.

Trust your intuition—and don't ever doubt that Spirit is working with you.

CHAPTER 15 Closing Thoughts

You do not have to be good.
You do not have to walk on your knees
For a hundred miles, through the desert,
repenting.
You only have to let the soft animal of your body
love what it loves.
Tell me about despair, yours, and I will tell you mine.
Meanwhile the world goes on.
Meanwhile the sun and the clear pebbles
of the rain
Are moving across the ladscapes,
over the prairies and the deep trees,
the mountains and the rivers.
Meanwhile the wild geese, high in the clean blue air
are heading home again.
Whoever you are, no matter how lonely,
The world offers itself to your imagination,
calls to you like the wild geese, harsh and
exciting—
over and over announcing your place
in the family of things/

Mary Oliver

The ancient Peruvians lived their lives practicing the wisdom of Ayni—the dance of life that includes gratitude for all things and reciprocity. They believed, according to Alex Stark, that Ayni affects everything. It comes from the human emotion of gratitude, which they believed kept reality in place. For Ayni to be manifested, knowledge of the self and your unique gifts must be cultivated and shared with your community. Further, the Peruvians believed that sharing is at the heart of giving. I am deeply grateful for the privilege of working with patients and their families as they prepared for their final transition. They shared the very essence of their lives- how Spirit touched them, and the wisdom, love, and values they gained from living their lives. My hope is that in sharing their stories with you, your own life may be immeasurably enhanced and deepened.

Just Beyond the Veil

BIBLIOGRAPHY

Longaker, Christine, Facing Death and Finding Hope Doubleday, 1997

Callanan, M, and P. Kelley, Final Gifts: Understanding the Special Awareness, Needs, and Communication of the Dying, New York: Posedion, 1992

Gerber, R, Vibrational Medicine: New Choices for Healing Ourselves. Santa Fe, NM, Bear and Company, 1998

Kubler –Ross, E On death And Dying. New York Mac-millan, 1969

Levine, S Who Dies?: An Investigation of Conscious Living and Conscious Dying, Garden City, NY, Anchor Books, 1982

Dowling Singh, Kathleen, The Grace in Dying, Harper Collins, NY, 2000

Chopra, Deepok, Life After Death, Random House, NY,2006

Boss, Pauline, Ambiguous Loss, Harvard College, 1999

Hays, Edward M., Prayers of a Planetary Pilgrim, Forest of Peace Books, Leavenworth, Ks, 1990

Feldman, Christine, Kornfield, Jack, Stories of the Spirit, Stories of the Heart, Harper Collins, Ny, 1991

Moody, Raymond Jr., Life After Life, New York, Bantam, 1975

Barrett, Ruth, Women's Rites, Women's Mysteries, Anchor House, 2004

Braden, Gregg, The Divine Matrix, Hay House, 2007

Braden, Gregg, Secrets of the Lost Mode of Prayer, Hay House, Carlsblad, Ca, 2006

Arrien, Angeles, The FourFold Way,

Berkus, Rusty, To Heal Again, Red Rose Press, Encino, Ca, 1986

Mindell, Arnold, Coma, Key to Awakening, Boston, Shambala, 1989

Roberts and Amidon, Earth Prayers, Jarper Collins, San Francisco, 1991

Berkus, Rusty, To Heal Again, Red Rose Press, 1986

Ladinsky, Daniel, the Subject Tonight is Love, 60 wild and sweet poems of Hafiz, Penguin Books, 1996

Starhawk, M Macha Nightmare and the Reclaiming Collective, Harper San Francisco, 1997 , The Pagan Book of Living and Dying: Practical Rituals, Prayers, Blessings, and Meditations of Crossing Over

Krishnamurti, J., The Book Of Life, Harper Collins, 1995 *Suggested Reading*

ABOUT DYING

Final Gifts: Understanding the Special Awareness, Needs, and Communication of the Dying, by Maggie Callanan and Patricia Kelley (1997 , Bantam Books)

Who Dies: An Investigation of Conscious Living and Conscious Dying , by Stephen Levine (1982 , ASnchor Books)

Tuesdays with Morrie: An Old man, a Young Man, and Life's Greatest Lesson ,by Mitch Albom (1997, Doubleday)

Living into Dying: A journal of Spiritual and Practical Deathcare for Family and Community, by Salli Rasberry and Carol Rae Watanbe (2001, Celestial Arts)

The Illuminated Rumi, Coleman Barks and Michael Green, Broadway Books, New York Ny, 1997

Selected Poems of Ranier Maria Rilke, Harper and Row, New York, NY 1981

FOR CAREGIVERS

May I Walk you Home: Courage and Comfort for Caregivers of the Very Ill, Stories by Joyce Hutchison, Prayers by Joyce Rupp

\Share The Care: How to Organize a Group to Care for Someone Who is Seriously Ill, by Cappy Capossela and Sheila Warnock

ABOUT CREATING RIUAL FOR EMBRACING THE END OF LIFE

Sacred Dying: Creating Rituals for Embracing the End of Life, by Megory Anderson (20001